SURVIVING THE RIVER

Louise Spilsbury

 Gareth Stevens
PUBLISHING

Please visit our website, www.garethstevens.com.
For a free color catalog of all our high-quality books,
call toll free 1-800-542-2595 or fax 1-877-542-2596.

CATALOGING-IN-PUBLICATION DATA

Names: Spilsbury, Louise.
Title: Surviving the river / Louise Spilsbury.
Description: New York : Gareth Stevens Publishing, 2017. | Series: Sole survivor |
    Includes index.
Identifiers: ISBN 9781482450750 (pbk.) | ISBN 9781482450774 (library bound) |
    ISBN 9781482450767 (6 pack)
Subjects: LCSH: Survival--Juvenile literature. | Survival skills--Juvenile literature. |
    Rivers--Juvenile literature.
Classification: LCC GV200.5 S65 2017| DDC 613.69--dc23

First Edition

Published in 2017 by
Gareth Stevens Publishing
111 East 14th Street, Suite 349
New York, NY 10003

Copyright © 2017 Gareth Stevens Publishing

Produced for Gareth Stevens by Calcium
Editors: Sarah Eason and Jennifer Sanderson
Designer: Paul Myerscough

Picture credits: Cover: Shutterstock: Anze Bizjan (right), Sergey Uryadnikov (left).
Inside: Shutterstock: Koldunov Alexey 14–15, Poprotskiy Alexey 21, Baciu 38–39,
Bikeriderlondon 42–43, Bildagentur Zoonar GmbH 16, Blend Images 5, Richard
Chaff 36–37, M. Cornelius 30–31, Cuson 26–27, Elaine Davis 37, Timothy Epp 15,
Except Else 11, Anton Gvozdikov 18–19, Mat Hayward 16–17, Heiko Kiera 28–29,
D. Kucharski K. Kucharska 22–23, Dudarev Mikhail 8–9, Jens Ottoson 20–21,
Pecold 1, 34–35, Photo Image 4–5, Gunnar Rathbun 10–11, Scott Sanders 12–13,
Jack Scott 40–41, Martijn Smeets 32–33, Smileimage9 24–25, Aleksey Stemmer
13, Samo Trebizan 30, Suzanne Tucker 6–7.

Printed in the United States of America
CPSIA compliance information: Batch #CS16GS:
For further information contact Gareth Stevens, New York, New York at 1-800-542-2595.

CONTENTS

Chapter One

RIVER DANGERS

Rivers are constantly on the move. That is what makes them exciting. It is also what makes them dangerous. Every year thousands of people are injured or drown while crossing, swimming, or boating in rivers. No two rivers are the same. Rivers may be shallow but fast-moving, or slow but deep. Some are narrow and some very wide.

In the middle of the Mississippi River, people can be a mile away from the shore.

Rivers usually start in mountains and hills, and flow toward oceans, lakes, or other rivers. Their water comes from rain or melted snow, or it can come from a **spring** under the land. Rivers flow downhill and across flatter land. On slopes, rivers tend to move very quickly and waters can be rough. On flatter land, rivers slow down but here rivers can be very deep and equally deadly.

Exploring rivers in a group is a good idea because it means people can help each other if needed.

How to Survive

Before setting out on any river adventure, people should understand what dangers they might face and learn what to do in order to survive. There are some basic rules everyone should follow:

- Plan the trip carefully.
- Check the weather and river conditions before setting off.
- Ensure that they have all the equipment they need and that it all works properly.
- Tell someone where they are going and when they should be back.
- Visit rivers as part of a group because there is safety in numbers.

In this book we are going to look at some of the hazards people face on rivers and how some people have survived the most terrifying disasters of all.

Read each page carefully—there are a lot of survival tips and some great information that will help you correctly answer the Do or Die questions. You can find the answers on pages 44 and 45.

SINK OR SWIM

One of the greatest dangers people face in a river is drowning. Anyone can get into trouble while swimming in a river. The water may be rough or their feet may become tangled in weeds on the riverbed. People also drown if their canoe or boat **capsizes** and they find themselves thrown suddenly into deep or quick-moving water. Some people have found themselves in rivers after their aircraft crash-landed.

If a boat capsizes, people should grab onto the boat and paddle. Light boats such as kayaks can wash away very quickly, so it is important to move fast.
If there is no boat, or the boat is lost, people should still try to grab onto something to help them float. Otherwise, river **currents** can drag people under or farther away from the shore.

"I SURVIVED..."

JOSEPH ASHALLEY WAS DRIVING ACROSS A BRIDGE ONE NIGHT WHEN THE BRIDGE COLLAPSED AND HIS TRUCK CRASHED INTO THE DEEP RIVER BELOW. ASHALLEY ROSE TO THE SURFACE BUT SANK AGAIN. THE NEXT TIME HE CAME UP GASPING FOR AIR, HE MANAGED TO GRAB A TREE BRANCH. FOR HOURS HE AVOIDED DROWNING BY HOLDING ONTO THE BRANCH. FINALLY, HIS SCREAMS WERE HEARD AND HE WAS PULLED TO SAFETY ON A LONG ROPE.

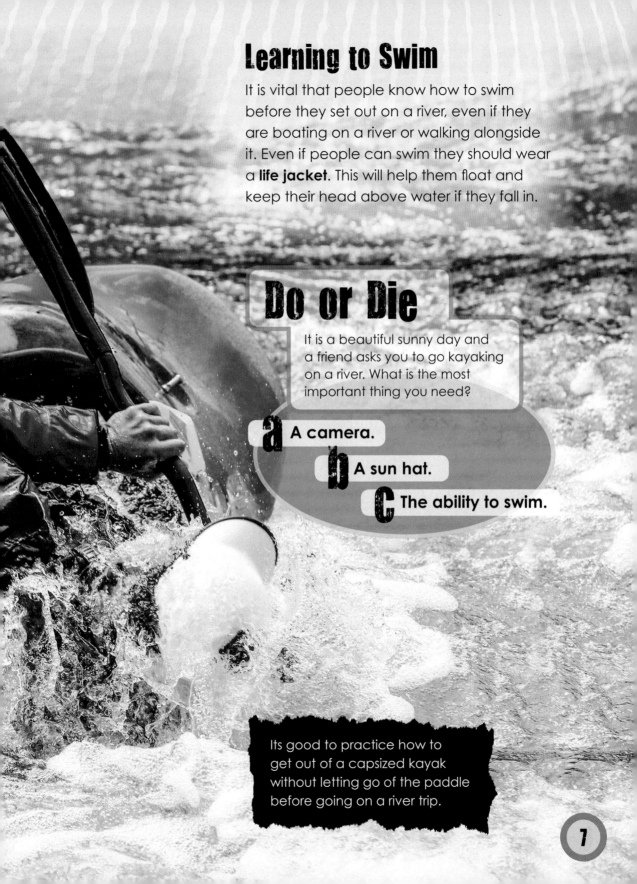

Learning to Swim

It is vital that people know how to swim before they set out on a river, even if they are boating on a river or walking alongside it. Even if people can swim they should wear a **life jacket**. This will help them float and keep their head above water if they fall in.

Do or Die

It is a beautiful sunny day and a friend asks you to go kayaking on a river. What is the most important thing you need?

a A camera.

b A sun hat.

c The ability to swim.

Its good to practice how to get out of a capsized kayak without letting go of the paddle before going on a river trip.

COLD WATERS

The water in rivers is often cold. This is partly because river water is flowing all the time so the water does not stay in one place long enough to **absorb** heat to warm up. Jumping into a cold river can be a great way to cool down on a summer's day. However, if people fall into cold river water and cannot get out quickly enough, they can become so cold they get **hypothermia**. Hypothermia can be deadly.

Hypothermia is a condition in which the body becomes so cold it cannot work properly and starts to shut down. Symptoms include becoming confused and sleepy. If left untreated, people can die. It is vital that people get out of cold water as soon as they feel cold. They should change out of wet clothes and warm up as quickly as they can.

Make a Fire

If people are lost in a remote part of a river and do not have dry clothes, they should make a fire. There are usually trees growing in the soil near a river so their sticks and branches can be used to build a fire.

Using dry wood for a fire will help it catch light more quickly than using damp wood.

Do or Die

You are kayaking down a river when the boat capsizes and washes away. You manage to get to the riverbank but you are freezing. Is the first thing you do:

a Remove your wet clothes and put on dry ones?

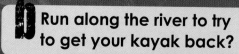

b Run along the river to try to get your kayak back?

c Try to find food?

SHELTER

If a boat capsizes and people are stranded by a river, the first thing they should do is get warm and dry. Most urgently, they will need to build a shelter. A shelter protects people from wind and rain. In hot places, it will also protect them from the sun during the day. Shelters keep out dangerous **predators** that might visit the river, too.

It is important to choose a safe site in which to build a shelter. Too close to the river, there is a danger of **flooding**. There is also a danger of being bitten or stung by insects if the shelter is too close to the river. People should also avoid rotting trees and overhanging rocks.

Sleeping in a hammock is one way to rest above the ground away from damp and biting insects.

Building Materials

A temporary shelter can be very simple. Ideally, it should have steep sides so the rain washes off it. Making it small—just big enough to lie in—helps keep the shelter warm. People could simply lean branches against a rock or tree, covered with leaves, to form a room.

Off the Ground

When sleeping, it is best to keep off the ground. Lying directly on soil can make people cold. There is also the risk of insects and bugs crawling out of the soil into a bed. It is possible to make a mat from leaves, branches, and moss. This will raise people off the ground while they sleep and **insulate** them from the cold ground.

The roof of this shelter slopes in the middle. If rain collects in the dip, the shelter may collapse.

Do or Die

Your boat capsizes and you make it to shore, but night is closing in. You need to make a shelter. Will you build it:

a On the riverbank?

b Under an old tree?

c In a clearing against a low, solid rock?

Chapter Two

FOOD AND DRINK

When people set out on a river adventure, they usually take supplies of food and water with them. Rivers contain freshwater that should be safe to drink. However, some rivers are **polluted** so it is not always safe to drink the water. It is always safest to pack plenty of supplies before setting out, but survivors can find food to eat in and around rivers if they know where to look.

People can eat plants growing alongside rivers, but they must know which ones are safe. Eating the wrong plant can lead to sickness or even death. The rule is never to pick or eat anything unless certain what it is. That is why taking a guide to help to identify plants can be very useful.

Recognizing Plants

Some easily recognizable plants grow by water. Watercress grows in streams and rivers. This leafy green plant has a peppery taste. Dandelions grow on some riverbanks and can be eaten as a salad. Sweet, juicy cranberries grow on long vines in sandy marshes near water.

It is best to cook wild watercress before eating it to kill off any tiny worm **larvae** that can make people very sick.

Rice

In some places, people might find wild rice growing in slow-flowing streams or the wet land on a riverbank. Rice plants grow only in standing water. The rice grains people eat are the seeds that grow in the flowering heads of the plants that grow above the water at the top of long stems. When rice grains are cooked, they are healthy and filling.

People can eat fresh cranberries straight from the plant, but they taste a little sour.

Do or Die

Your food supplies fell off your boat and washed away. When you pull into the bank for the night you are hungry. Do you eat:

a Red berries because they look sweet?

b Watercress because it is the only plant you recognize?

c Some flowers because they remind you of a plant at home?

WATER

Some rivers are polluted by chemical waste that is dumped from factories that are built near the river upstream. Others are polluted by **fertilizers** and other farm waste that rain washes off fields, and into streams and rivers. Garbage is another form of pollution. Sometimes an animal falls into a river and dies and its rotting body pollutes the water, too.

Finding freshwater to drink is one of the most important things survivors must do. People can last for several weeks without food but for only three days without water. However, drinking polluted water can cause stomachache, **diarrhea**, or vomiting. In the very worst cases, **contaminated** water can be fatal. Even crystal-clear mountain water can contain millions of **microorganisms** people cannot see.

Boiling water for about five to 10 minutes on a high, rolling boil should make it safe to drink.

"I SURVIVED..."

WHEN MIYUKI HARWOOD FELL AND BROKE HER LEG AND ANKLE, AND DAMAGED HER SPINE, SHE COULD NOT WALK. SHE KNEW SHE HAD TO GET WATER TO SURVIVE. SHE MANAGED TO SURVIVE ONLY BECAUSE SHE SPENT DAYS CRAWLING TO A RIVER. THERE, SHE WAS ABLE TO USE A WATER **FILTER** TO MAKE 2 PINTS (1 L) OF FRESHWATER EVERY DAY. DRINKING THIS KEPT HER ALIVE UNTIL RESCUERS FOUND HER.

Cleaning Water

Before drinking water, people should treat it to kill any harmful substances in it. One of the best methods of treating water is to boil it. If survivors do not have a stove, they could make a fire to do this. They can also use a water filter or special tablets that purify the water.

Do or Die

You have been walking through a forest when at last you come to a river. You are desperately thirsty. Do you:

a Drink straight from the river?

b Pour water through a sieve to remove pieces of dirt you see?

c Boil the water first?

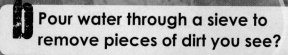

This hiker is pumping water through a filter to make it clean and safe to drink.

CATCHING FISH

Most rivers are full of fish, and these animals make a tasty, filling meal if survivors can catch them. Fish have a number of **adaptations** to help them live their whole lives underwater. They breathe **underwater using** special body parts called **gills**. They swim by moving their bodies from side to side. They have **fins** that help them stay upright in the water, to brake and to steer.

Fish also have a smooth **streamlined** shape, a little like a torpedo. This enables them to move through flowing water more easily. It also helps them swim upstream against a fast current. Salmon swim upstream to lay their eggs in rivers and they can even jump up waterfalls.

Types of Fish

Different kinds of fish live in different types of river. Bass usually live in slow-moving rivers. Trout usually live in cool, clear, fast-moving water. Some river fish, such as piranha, are dangerous and give a nasty bite. It is important to know which are safe to catch.

It is best to cook fish before eating it to make sure it is safe to eat.

Catching Fish

It is safer to catch fish from the shore or in shallow water. If people wade in too deep, they might be washed away. To find fish, people should look for calm areas of a river where there are weeds. Fish often shelter or lay eggs in weeds. To catch fish, people can make a net from a piece of fabric and hold that underwater. They can also sharpen the ends of a strong, straight stick to make a spear.

It can be possible to catch salmon as they swim in a river.

Do or Die

You are lost near a river and you have run out of the food supplies you brought with you. The best place to catch some fish to eat is:

a In fast-moving water?

b In the deep middle part of the river?

c In calm water among weeds?

Chapter Three

CROSSING RIVERS

There comes a point on almost every trip along a river when hikers, boaters, or explorers need to cross the water. This is not a problem on narrow, shallow rivers with gently flowing waters. People can wade across these easily. However, crossing a river that is very deep or has a fast-moving current can be dangerous. People can drown or be thrown against hard rocks by rough waters.

Before setting out on any river trip, adventurers should research the river they are visiting. They should learn which parts of the river might be dangerous, where it is deep, and where they might meet hazards. They should check the weather forecast, too. Heavy rain can swell rivers, making them dangerous because they flow faster.

Choosing the safest place to cross a river can make the difference between life and death.

Keeping Safe

Knowing as much as possible about rivers helps keep people safe. For example, people should know that wet rocks, especially those covered in **algae**, are slippery. Trying to walk or climb over these rocks can lead to a fall. However, rocks that are high above the water's surface and are dry might make good stepping-stones across some rivers.

Currents

Judging the depth and speed of water is a vital skill. Even shallow water, if it is moving fast, can carry people away. In general, the shallower or narrower a riverbed becomes, the faster its water flows. Wide, deep rivers usually flow more slowly. People should always throw a stick into the water to see how quickly it moves. People should never get into water that is moving faster than they can swim.

Do or Die

The path you are following along a river leads to an obstacle. You need to cross to the other side. There are some rocks across the water. Do you:

a Check that they are dry?

b Walk across them even though they are wet?

c Walk across them even though they are covered in algae?

WHERE TO CROSS

Before attempting to cross a river, people should locate a safe and easy place to cross it. The best way to do this is to find a high point, with a good view over a long stretch of the river or stream. This could be from a tree, up a hill, or on top of a rock. From this vantage point, people can look for a safe place to cross.

From the vantage point, things to look for include a level part of the river where it breaks into several **channels**. It is easier to cross two or three narrow channels than a wide river. It is also good to pick a place upstream from a bank or **sandbar**. These natural barriers will keep people from being washed downstream if they become caught in a current.

"I SURVIVED..."

JEZ BRAGG NEARLY LOST HIS LIFE WHEN HE ATTEMPTED TO CROSS A RIVER. INSTEAD OF WAITING TO FIND A CALM SPOT TO CROSS, HE ATTEMPTED TO CROSS A VERY STEEP, FLOODED, AND FAST-FLOWING RIVER. HE WAS WASHED AWAY AND KNOCKED AGAINST THE ROCKS. HE MANAGED TO STAY ABOVE THE SURFACE AND EVENTUALLY MADE IT TO THE OTHER SIDE. LATER, HE ADMITTED IT WAS A CLOSE CALL AND HE HAD THOUGHT HIS TIME WAS UP.

Across the River

It is also important to look across the river to check there is an easy way to get out of the water on the other side. If there is a high bank that will be difficult to climb, it is better to go back upstream to an easier crossing site.

Another way to cross a dangerous river is using a rope stretched from one side to the other above the water.

It is usually safest to cross a river at the point where it is wide and shallow.

Do or Die

You have to cross a river and you have climbed to a high point to choose the best route. Which of these three options is best? Is it:

a A level part of the river where it breaks into several channels?

b A stretch of river with high banks on either side?

c A place downstream of a sandbar?

21

Chapter Four

ANIMAL ATTACKS

There are a variety of animals living in rivers and along riverbanks. Some are harmless but others are incredibly dangerous. Goliath tigerfish live up to their name. These monster fish are fierce predators. They have 32 razor-sharp teeth that are as big as those of a great white shark. They hunt in packs and eat large animals such as crocodiles. Attacks on humans by goliath tigerfish are rare, but they have happened.

The diving bell spider is the only spider that lives underwater its whole life. It forms a bubble of air that it holds between hairs on its legs. It uses this to breathe underwater in slow-moving streams. It eats insect larvae and other water spiders. Diving bell spiders can give people a painful bite that can cause a fever, too.

Stingrays

Freshwater stingrays live in rivers in Southeast Asia and Australia. They can grow to 16.5 feet (5 m) long. They are hard to spot because they bury themselves in sand and mud on the riverbed. Stingrays have a stinger at the end of their tail that contains deadly poison.

Staying Alert

The only sure way to survive an encounter with a dangerous river animal is never to meet one in the first place! Before going on a river adventure, learn where dangerous animals live and stay away. If people are in a river **habitat** where dangerous animals might be found, they must stay alert at all times. If people see a potentially dangerous animal they should stay calm and leave the area immediately.

The diving bell spider has venomous fangs that are sharp enough to pierce human skin!

Do or Die

You are swimming in the Amazon River and you see the shadow of an animal lurking nearby. Do you:

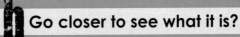

a Swim calmly but quickly back to shore?

b Go closer to see what it is?

c Splash the water to get its attention?

HIPPOS

Hippopotamuses look like gentle giants. They are usually found wallowing in slow-moving rivers and lakes in Africa. In fact, hippos are one of the most dangerous and aggressive of all animals. They have huge teeth that grow up to 20 inches (50 cm) long. They usually use these for fighting or to scare off enemies. A hippo can kill people who make it feel threatened or to protect its young.

Hippos are adapted for life in the river. Their eyes, ears, and nostrils are on the top of the head, so they can hear, see, and breathe while their body is under the water. They do not swim. Instead, they walk on the riverbed with their **webbed** toes. They rest, usually in the water, during the day, and at night they come out of the water to feed.

People should take great care when near hippos because these animals can be aggressive.

Hippo Attack

To avoid attack, do not walk between a hippo and the river. The hippo may become scared and attack. Take care not to nudge hippos with a paddle when in a boat because this can anger them. Avoid hippo areas at night, when these animals are most active. If a hippo attacks, run as fast as you can away from the water.

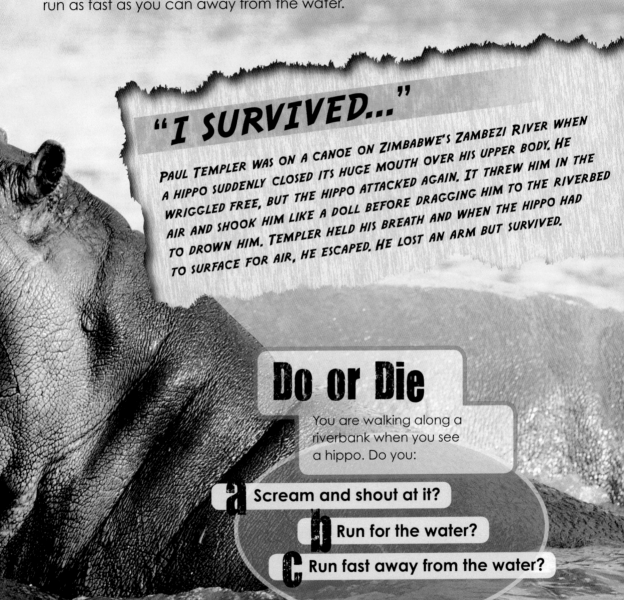

"I SURVIVED..."

PAUL TEMPLER WAS ON A CANOE ON ZIMBABWE'S ZAMBEZI RIVER WHEN A HIPPO SUDDENLY CLOSED ITS HUGE MOUTH OVER HIS UPPER BODY. HE WRIGGLED FREE, BUT THE HIPPO ATTACKED AGAIN. IT THREW HIM IN THE AIR AND SHOOK HIM LIKE A DOLL BEFORE DRAGGING HIM TO THE RIVERBED TO DROWN HIM. TEMPLER HELD HIS BREATH AND WHEN THE HIPPO HAD TO SURFACE FOR AIR, HE ESCAPED. HE LOST AN ARM BUT SURVIVED.

Do or Die

You are walking along a riverbank when you see a hippo. Do you:

a Scream and shout at it?

b Run for the water?

c Run fast away from the water?

ELECTRIC EELS

Electric eels are river animals that can deliver an electric shock that is powerful enough to **paralyze** a horse! They use an electrical **charge** to knock out **prey** and to deter any predators that try to attack them. It is rare for a human to die from an electric eel attack, but it has happened. People can drown after being stunned. Repeated shocks can keep people from breathing or cause a heart attack.

An electric eel has electrocytes all over its body. These special body parts store power like tiny batteries. All of the electrolytes can release an electric charge at the same time. This acts like a stun gun. It knocks out prey such as other fish. The eel then sucks victims into its mouth. It can also scare away predators, such as small alligator-like animals called caiman.

Electric eels, which are actually a type of catfish, swim about in the murky waters of the Amazon River.

Shocking!

Electric eels are not vicious. They do not chase people. They usually avoid such large animals. However, they will attack if they feel threatened. People who live along the Amazon River even avoid eating electric eels because the eels can give off shocks eight hours after they die!

Avoid Attack

The only way to avoid an electric eel is to stay out of waters where they live. Electric eels swim in the murky streams of the Amazon River. This makes them difficult to see, even if people keep a lookout for them. If someone does go into water in which electric eels live, they should get out as soon as they feel a shock, in case the eel repeats the attack.

Do or Die

It is a burning hot day in the Amazon and you need a swim to cool down. You find yourself near a murky stretch of river where there might be electric eels. Should you:

a Swim with a friend—there is safety in numbers?

b Stay out of the water?

c Just paddle in the water?

ALLIGATORS

Alligators live in and around slow-moving water that has a lot of mud and plants. They eat turtles, fish, and animals such as deer. Alligators will eat almost anything they can find, and they have been known to eat people! They grab prey in their jaws, which are powerful enough to crush even a hard turtle shell. These reptiles swallow small prey whole. They drag larger prey into the water, drown it, and then eat it.

To catch prey, alligators drift along in the water as if they were a floating log. Their eyes, ears, and nostrils are raised on their heads. This means that when the rest of their body is under the water, they can still breathe and see above the water. When they get close, they attack.

"I SURVIVED..."

IN 2011, DAVID BOSTWICK WAS SWIMMING IN FLORIDA WHEN AN ALLIGATOR SUDDENLY ATTACKED AND CLAMPED ITS JAWS DOWN ON HIS HEAD. BOSTWICK GRABBED HOLD OF THE ALLIGATOR'S JAWS WITH HIS HANDS AND USED ALL HIS STRENGTH TO FORCE OPEN THE BEAST'S MOUTH. AFTER A FEW MOMENTS' STRUGGLE, THE ALLIGATOR FINALLY RELEASED HIM. BOSTWICK WAS TAKEN TO THE HOSPITAL WHERE HE NEEDED 50 STITCHES.

Keeping Safe

Alligators are slower on land than in water, so if one attacks on land, people should run away from the animal as quickly as they can. If they fall into water where alligators live, they should not splash or shout as this might make the alligators attack. People should swim or walk to safety quickly, but calmly and quietly.

Do or Die

You are on a canoe in a river when the boat capsizes and you find yourself in alligator-infested water. Do you:

a Shout loudly for help?

b Kick your legs to scare alligators away?

c Swim or walk to safety calmly, quietly, and quickly?

Alligators can hold their breath for up to 30 minutes when underwater.

Chapter Five

RIVER HAZARDS

No two river parts of a river are the same. Rivers vary greatly along their length. While a river might be calm and gentle at one point, it can quickly become a raging torrent. When currents change, they can make kayakers lose control or capsize boats in deep stretches of water. People have also built structures along rivers that can cause hazards, such as **dams**.

The water around dams looks calm and gentle, but it is very dangerous. There is a real risk of people in a boat getting caught in the raging water that drops over the dam. If this happens, they are pulled under by the rolling water and it is then almost impossible for them to get out.

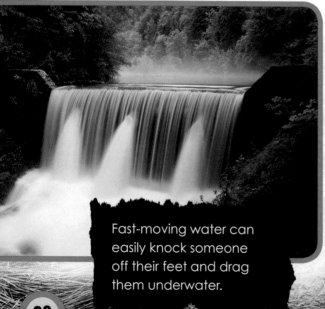

Fast-moving water can easily knock someone off their feet and drag them underwater.

Danger at Estuaries

Estuaries are areas of flat, wide water where rivers meet the sea. They often look easy to cross, but they can flow quickly and be dangerous. They also change with the tides, and tides can cause currents, even upstream from the estuary mouth.

Plan Ahead

Before going on any river trip, people should figure out a plan of action for any emergency that might occur. This could include the boat capsizing or one person becoming separated from the rest of his or her group. If the worst happens, the most important thing is not to panic. If people panic, they cannot think clearly. They might forget their action plan and put themselves at even greater risk.

Do or Die

A friend asks you to go boating on the river. You have a choice of three places to go. Do you choose near:

a A dam?

b An estuary?

c A calm stretch of river?

People can become stuck in the deep, soft mud in estuaries. If this happens, they could drown when the tide comes in.

WATERFALLS

Waterfalls are places along a river where the water suddenly flows over a steep ledge of rock into a pool below. Waterfalls form where a layer of hard rock sits above softer rock. The river **erodes** the soft rock, creating a ledge. Waterfalls are beautiful to look at so they are popular places for people to visit. However, they can also be very dangerous.

The water at the top of a waterfall can look calm. This tempts people to wade in it or possibly to look over the ledge. This is when accidents happen. People can slip on wet rocks, slide down steep slopes, or get caught in strong currents and be pulled over the ledge. Waterfalls can be very high and the pools at the bottom are often full of rocks.

Waterfall Safety

If people visit waterfalls they should follow these safety rules:
- Never try to cross a river above or even close to waterfalls.
- Stay away from the top of waterfalls.
- Never climb waterfalls.
- Do not jump off waterfalls.
- Avoid slippery rocks.
- Watch where they step.
- Stay out of restricted areas.

Do or Die

You visit a waterfall for a picnic with friends. Is it safe to:

a Climb the waterfall?

 Jump off the waterfall?

 Watch the waterfall from land around the pool at its base?

"I SURVIVED..."

When 17-year-old Patrick Owens walked to a waterfall in 2014, he ignored warning signs and climbed to the pool above the falls. He became caught in the current and was swept over the waterfall. He landed on rocks 90 feet (274 m) below. He woke up four days later in the hospital. He now has to use a wheelchair to get around, but he said he knew he was lucky to be alive.

It is safer to view a waterfall from the base—the best views are almost always from there, too.

RAPIDS

Rapids are areas of shallow, fast-moving water in a river or stream. They happen where water flowing over the land has been able to erode softer rocks, and harder rocks have been left behind. When water flows over these remaining rocks and boulders, they break up the flow of the stream. This makes the river water so rough it easily tips over boats or drags swimmers into rocks.

People have great fun riding over rapids in boats but they should do so only with the help of an experienced guide. They should also avoid the more dangerous rapids. Rapids are graded according to how dangerous they are. Lowest-grade rapids have only small waves and no obstacles. The most dangerous rapids have strong waves, lots of obstacles, fast currents, and waterfalls.

Be Safe

If rafting through rapids, people should wear protective equipment. They need helmets in case they fall out and hit a rock. They should make sure a rescue kayaker accompanies them. He or she will be able scoop out survivors from the water if they get into trouble.

White-water rafting is thrilling but it's important to wear the correct safety gear while doing this sport.

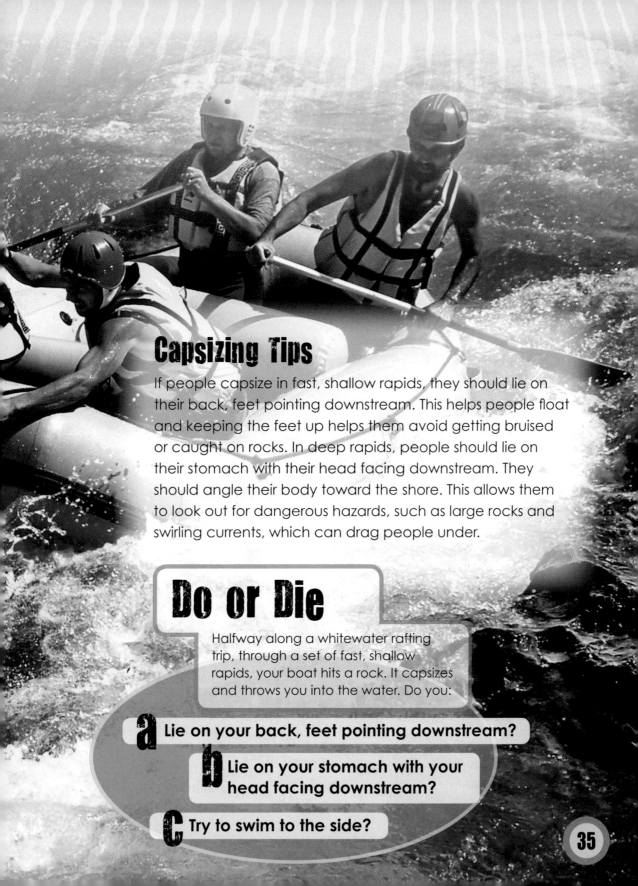

Capsizing Tips

If people capsize in fast, shallow rapids, they should lie on their back, feet pointing downstream. This helps people float and keeping the feet up helps them avoid getting bruised or caught on rocks. In deep rapids, people should lie on their stomach with their head facing downstream. They should angle their body toward the shore. This allows them to look out for dangerous hazards, such as large rocks and swirling currents, which can drag people under.

Do or Die

Halfway along a whitewater rafting trip, through a set of fast, shallow rapids, your boat hits a rock. It capsizes and throws you into the water. Do you:

a Lie on your back, feet pointing downstream?

b Lie on your stomach with your head facing downstream?

c Try to swim to the side?

EDDIES AND WHIRLPOOLS

Eddies happen in rivers where rocks, bends, or other obstacles push water in the opposite direction to the main flow. This creates what looks like a calm spot of water. When a kayak hits an eddy, the sudden change in flow direction can easily flip over the boat and throw passengers into the water. Eddies can trap and toss a boat or kayak around as if it were a toy.

Eddies and whirlpools can take canoeists and kayakers by surprise and drag them under.

Sometimes, violent eddies form whirlpools. Whirlpools are areas where the water flows in downward circles or spirals. Most whirlpools are not very powerful. Small whirlpools may just spin a kayak around for a few moments. Big whirlpools are dangerous because they can suck boats and people under the water.

"I SURVIVED..."

IT WAS DARK WHEN KEVIN STRAIN'S BOAT HIT SOME ROCKS AND CAPSIZED IN A FAST-MOVING RIVER. KEVIN WAS NOT WEARING A LIFE JACKET. A STRONG CURRENT CARRIED HIM FOR THREE HOURS THROUGH AT LEAST FOUR WHIRLPOOLS. EACH WHIRLPOOL DRAGGED HIM DOWN, BUT HE CLUNG TO TWO EMPTY GAS CANS THAT WERE THROWN INTO THE WATER WITH HIM SO THAT HE COULD KEEP COMING UP TO BREATHE. FINALLY, HE WASHED UP ON A SHORE AND HELP ARRIVED.

When someone sees a large whirlpool in a river they should steer a course around it.

Avoiding Disaster

People can avoid eddies and whirlpools by kayaking or canoeing around them. They can get out of the water and drag their boat along the shore until they are past the danger. If caught in a whirlpool, paddling strongly to the side heading downstream should propel people out of it.

Do or Die

You are kayaking down a river of rapids when you see a whirlpool ahead. You cannot avoid it. Is it safest to:

a Paddle straight into it?

b Paddle to the side of the whirlpool heading downstream?

c Paddle to the side and drag the boat along the shore until you are past it?

Chapter Six

ESCAPE!

When people have found the food and water they need to survive, they can start to think about how to find their way home. This is easier if people have **navigation** equipment such as a **compass** or **global positioning system (GPS)**. If people are completely lost, their best chance is to follow a river downstream. Rivers and streams often lead to villages or towns.

People could walk along the riverbank. If the river is safe to travel on, they could float downstream. One way to do this is by filling an item of clothing, such as a pair of pants, with air, and tie the ends so the clothing floats. By holding it, people can float along. The other option is to make a raft.

Do or Die

After leaving your group to explore on a mountain river trip, you find yourself lost. You have no navigation equipment. Do you:

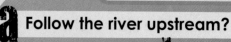

a Follow the river upstream?

b Follow the river downstream?

c Walk away from the river?

Make a Raft

One way to make raft is to lay four or five long logs side by side. People should try to choose well-matched logs so that they make a level surface when tied together. They should tie two poles at both ends of the logs. There should be one above and one below each end of the logs. The poles should be tied together with vines so they trap the logs tightly between them.

Launch the Raft

Before getting in a raft, it is best to find a high point and check that the route ahead is safe. Carrying a long pole or paddle helps people steer and push off any obstacles the raft might otherwise crash into. People should then tie their belongings to the raft so they do not get washed away.

A wooden raft can be a safe and stable way to travel along a river.

RESCUE

Many trees and other plants grow in the rich, damp soil alongside a river. Their long roots grow deep down to keep them from getting washed away in floods. The roots help hold together a riverbank, too. In narrow rivers, tree leaves and branches make it difficult for rescuers in helicopters to see survivors below. If people hear a rescue helicopter, it is best to get to a clearing so that rescuers can see them.

People can send signals to rescuers from open spaces near a river. They can spell out the word HELP in stones from the riverbed. They can light a fire. If the smoke rises above the trees, people can see fires from far away.

Flares only burn for a short time so should not be lit until rescuers are nearby.

Making a Noise

When traveling on boats, people should always take a whistle or horn. This can be used to warn other boaters to move out of the way and avoid a crash. Whistles can also be used to call for help. People should also carry flares or other signaling devices, such as a mirror, that can be used to send signals in the dark.

"I SURVIVED..."

MALACHI BRADLEY WAS TEN YEARS OLD WHEN HE BECAME LOST DURING A HIKE WITH HIS FAMILY. HE SURVIVED A NIGHT BY CURLING UP BETWEEN ROCKS THAT WERE STILL WARM FROM THE SUN. HE DRANK RIVER WATER AND TRIED TO MAKE A SPEAR TO CATCH A FISH. WHEN HE HEARD A SEARCH HELICOPTER FLYING OVERHEAD, HE RAN TO A CLEARING AND WAITED. THIS MADE IT EASIER FOR THE PILOT TO SPOT HIM. HE WAS RESCUED SOON AFTER.

Do or Die

You have been lost for three days and you are resting under some trees close to a river. You hear a rescue helicopter in the distance. Is your next move to:

a Start to gather together your equipment and other belongings?

b Start shouting?

c Run to a clearing so the helicopter can see you?

BE PREPARED

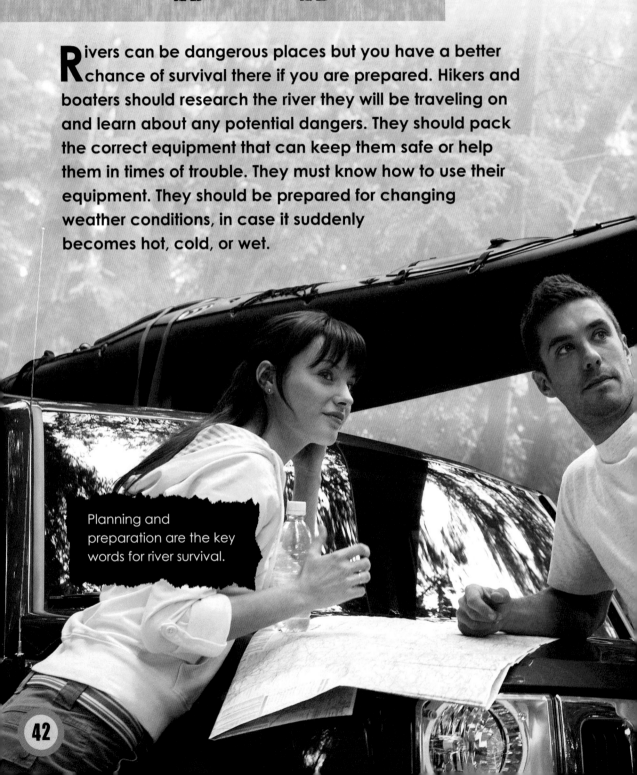

Rivers can be dangerous places but you have a better chance of survival there if you are prepared. Hikers and boaters should research the river they will be traveling on and learn about any potential dangers. They should pack the correct equipment that can keep them safe or help them in times of trouble. They must know how to use their equipment. They should be prepared for changing weather conditions, in case it suddenly becomes hot, cold, or wet.

Planning and preparation are the key words for river survival.

If traveling by boat, people should check their boat and other equipment before they leave. They should take the tools they need to repair the boat if it is damaged. Carrying a spare paddle and an extra life jacket is also a good idea. They should also wear their life jacket at all times. Life jackets work only when people wear them.

Safe Hiking

It also pays to be prepared when planning a walking trip near a river. Many river accidents are slips, trips, and falls that happen on the riverbank. People should choose hiking boots or sandals that provide good grip on wet rocks and slippery banks. They should watch where they are walking and avoid taking risks.

The Perfect Pack

Finally, people should pack their equipment, food, and first aid kit in a waterproof bag. If this is sealed tightly, it will protect its contents if it is tossed overboard. Even if the bag is washed away, if it is waterproof, it will protect the contents until people can retrieve it later. This could make the difference between life and death.

Do or Die

You have been invited to go boating on a river trip for three days. You have your kit ready and it is time to go. Do you carry your gear in:

a An ordinary backpack?

b A waterproof bag?

c A grocery bag?

ANSWERS

Would you survive if you were on your own and stranded on a river? Check your answers against these correct ones to see if you know how to survive.

Pages 6–7
Answer: C

A life jacket can help people float, but you really should not go on or near rivers until you can swim properly.

Pages 8–9
Answer: A

Getting dry and warm is the number one priority when you get cold in river water. Otherwise, you risk hypothermia.

Pages 10–11
Answer: C

It is best to avoid riverbanks where you might be hit by a flood or bitten by insects. You should avoid rotting trees because branches might fall on you. Resting branches against a low, solid rock is ideal.

Pages 12–13
Answer: B

Only ever eat plants that you recognize and are 100 percent certain are safe to eat. If unsure, do not touch or eat them.

Pages 14–15
Answer: C

Never drink river water without purifying it first. Just removing the dirt you can see is not enough either. Water could contain millions of microorganisms so tiny you cannot see them.

Pages 16–17
Answer: C

Fast-moving or deep water is dangerous as it might wash you away. Fish are less likely to live in it, and they will be harder to catch, too.

Pages 18–19
Answer: A

Crossing wet or algae-covered rocks is dangerous because you can slip and injure yourself.

Pages 20–21
Answer: A

If you cross a river with high banks either side you might not be able to get out again. A sandbar is useful only if it is upstream of a current so it can keep you from being washed away.

Pages 22–23
Answer: A

Never take risks. If you are unsure what type of animal you have encountered, get out of the water. Splashing or getting closer makes animals feel threatened, and if they are dangerous, they might attack.

Pages 24–25
Answer: C

Hippos cannot run fast for long, so running away is your best chance of escape. Dodging between rocks and trees will slow down these huge animals.

Pages 26–27
Answer: B

Electric eels can swim in shallow water so could still attack if you disturb them by walking or swimming. Staying out of the water is the only way to be safe.

Pages 28–29
Answer: C

Avoid splashing and making loud noises as this will attract the alligators' attention and make them more likely to attack. Move away quietly.

Pages 30-31
Answer: C

Avoid dams as you might be pulled over the drop. Avoid estuaries because they can flow quickly and be dangerous. Keep to calm stretches of river, ideally where other people are boating, too.

Pages 32–33
Answer: C

Waterfalls can be deadly so people should never climb or jump off them. People have died doing these activities.

Pages 34–35
Answer: A

Floating feet-first on your back helps you stay afloat and allows you to kick off passing rocks so they do not hurt you.

Pages 36–37
Answer: B

If there is no way to get out of the water, you should paddle to the side of the whirlpool heading downstream, but it is safer to avoid whirlpools altogether.

Pages 38–39
Answer: B

If you are in a remote place, such as a mountain river habitat, there are more likely to be people living downstream.

Pages 40–41
Answer: C

People in a rescue helicopter will not be able to help you if they cannot see you. It is vital to get out of the shelter of the trees and into a clearing.

Pages 42–43
Answer: B

The chances of things getting wet on a river trip are high. Protect your gear by carrying it in a waterproof bag.

GLOSSARY

absorb to soak up

adaptations features that help an animal or plant survive in its habitat

algae living things that can make their own food using energy from sunlight

capsizes turns over in the water

channels grooves in the land along which streams or rivers run

charge a store of electrical energy

compass a device with a magnetized pointer that shows the direction of north

contaminated dirty with germs or poisonous

currents areas of water moving in one direction

dams large walls that hold back water and raise its level. The water behind dams forms reservoirs used to create electricity or water supplies

diarrhea a condition in which people go to the washroom often and their stools are very loose

erodes wears away

fertilizers substances used to help plants grow

filter to pass something, such as water, through a mesh to remove dirt

fins parts of a fish's body that help it swim, steer, or slow down

flooding the covering of an area of land that is usually dry by a large amount of water

gills body parts that allow fish to breathe underwater

global positioning system (GPS) a system that helps people find their location on a map

habitat a place in nature where animals live

hypothermia a condition in which the body gets too cold to function

insulate to keep heat or cold from moving from one place to another

larvae the young, often wormlike form of some animals

life jacket a jacket filled with air that helps people float on water

microorganisms living things so tiny we cannot see them

navigation finding one's way around

paralyze to make something unable to move

polluted made dirty or dangerous with harmful substances

predators animals that hunt and eat other animals

prey an animal that is hunted and eaten by other animals

sandbar a long, narrow, sandy bank

sleepwalks walks around and does other things while still asleep

spring a place where water from under the ground comes out onto land

streamlined a long, thin torpedo shape that moves easily through water

webbed having skin between the toes of the feet

FOR MORE INFORMATION

Books

Kalman, Bobbi. *Where on Earth Are Rivers?* (Explore the Continents). St. Catharines, ON: Crabtree Publishing Company, 2014.

Leonard, Job. *Fall River Lake Safety Book*. CreateSpace Independent, 2015.

Otsis, Nate. *Nols River Rescue Guide*. Mechanicsburg, PA: Stackpole Books, 2015.

Rushing Rivers (It's All About...). New York, NY: Kingfisher, 2016.

Websites

Discover more about rivers at:
https://online.kidsdiscover.com/unit/rivers

Investigate rivers at:
http://pbskids.org/dragonflytv/show/rivers.html

Find out how we use and manage rivers at:
http://wwf.panda.org/about_our_earth/about_freshwater/rivers/

Explore how rivers become polluted at:
http://kids.niehs.nih.gov/explore/pollute/riverstream.htm

Publisher's note to educators and parents: Our editors have carefully reviewed these websites to ensure that they are suitable for students. Many websites change frequently, however, and we cannot guarantee that a site's future contents will continue to meet our high standards of quality and educational value. Be advised that students should be closely supervised whenever they access the Internet.

INDEX